JuV 331.8 TAf 2008

SPANISH

P9-DWE-815

DATE DUE

WITHDRAWN

PRINTED IN U.S.A.

CARSON CITY LIBRARY
900 North Roop Street
Carson City, NV 89701
775-887-2244

DEC 09 2014

That's Not Fair!

Emma Tenayuca's struggle for justice

¡No Es Justo!

La lucha de Emma Tenayuca por la justicia

Written by Carmen Tafolla & Sharyll Teneyuca

Illustrated by Terry Ybáñez

Spanish translation by Carmen Tafolla. Translation editors: Celina Marroquín and Amalia Mondríguez, Ph.D.

WINGS PRESS
Since 1975

San Antonio, Texas
2008

To Emma, Sojourner,
César, María, Ernesto,
y a todos los que, como
ellos, luchan por la
justicia. – C.T.

To Gregory, Douglas,
and Charles, who in
the blink of an eye,
have become fine, just,
young men. -S.T.

1925 . . .

The little girl with the shining, black eyes walked eagerly to school. She passed a small shack that had no door. Inside, a baby was crying, as his mother tried to warm him with her thin arms and her thin shawl. The little girl knew they were cold, and her black eyes flashed.

She passed a boy, maybe four years old. In his hands were a few small pecans he was shelling and sharing with two younger brothers. They ate eagerly as if that was all they would have today. The little girl knew they were hungry, and again, her eyes flashed.

La muchachita de brillantes ojos negros caminaba entusiasmada hacia la escuela. Pasó una casucha sin puerta. Adentro, un bebé lloraba mientras su madre trataba de protegerlo del frío con sus brazos delgados y su rebozo muy gastado. La niña sabía que tenían frío, y sus ojos negros relampaguearon.

Ella pasó junto a un niño de quizá cuatro años, que en sus manos tenía unas nueces pequeñas que estaba pelando y compartiendo con sus hermanitos. Comían ansiosamente, como si fuera todo lo que tuvieran para ese día. La niña sabía que tenían hambre. Suspiró profundamente y otra vez destellaron sus ojos.

3

When she arrived at school, her teacher announced happily, "Emma, look! We have a new book to read today."

Emma loved to read! She had read every book in the classroom! But even as she pored over the new book, she kept remembering the children she had seen that morning.

Cuando llegó a la escuela, su maestra anunció: –¡Mira, Emma! ¡Tenemos un libro nuevo para leer hoy!

A Emma le encantaba leer. ¡Había leído todos los libros que había en el salón de clases! Pero aún mientras leía el nuevo libro, no podía dejar de pensar en los niños que había visto por la mañana.

NOVEMBER 1925

After school, she took the new book home. And read it again. And again. As she sat on the front porch reading, María, a neighbor about her age peeked over and asked, "What are you doing?"

"I'm reading a wonderful story! Would you like to read it, too?"

Después de las clases, se llevó el libro nuevo a su casa. Y lo leyó otra vez. Y otra. Se encontraba sentada en la veranda de su casa, cuando María, una vecinita de su edad se asomó y le preguntó:
—¿Qué haces?
—¡Estoy leyendo un cuento maravilloso! ¿Quieres leerlo?

"Oh, I can't!" said María. "I don't know how to read. Last year, I was starting to learn the letters. But then, the weather began to warm, and the flowers began to bloom. And my family had to go far away, to pick onions."

"We picked onions, then strawberries. We picked cabbage, then cotton. We picked beets, then corn. By the time we came back, school had ended, summer had passed, and school had started again."

8

—¡Oh, no puedo! —dijo María. —No sé leer. El año pasado estaba empezando a aprender las letras. Pero llegó el tiempo de calor y las plantas comenzaron a florecer y mi familia tuvo que irse lejos a piscar cebollas.

—Piscamos cebollas, y después fresas. Piscamos repollo, y después algodón. Piscamos betabel, y después helote. Cuando regresamos, las clases ya habían terminado, el verano ya se había pasado y la escuela había comenzado otra vez.

"When I went back to school, I was lost. Everyone already knew how to read. And I didn't. I had missed it!"

Emma's black eyes flashed like lightning in a black sky. "That's not fair!!"

María sighed, "Now I'm so far behind, I'll never learn to read."

Emma grew very quiet, and the little girl's words stayed inside her for a long time.

POEMS

LITERATURE

HISTORY

SCIENCE

MATH

—Cuando regresé a la escuela, me sentí perdida. Ya todos sabían leer. Y yo no. ¡Había perdido la oportunidad de aprender!

Los ojos de Emma brillaron como relámpagos en un cielo de noche oscura. —¡Eso no es justo! —murmuró.

María suspiró y dijo: —¡Ahora estoy tan atrasada, que nunca aprenderé a leer!

Emma se quedó muy callada, y las palabras de la muchachita se le quedaron adentro por mucho tiempo.

On Sunday afternoon, Emma went with Grandpa to the park. The air was crisp and cool. The sun was shining. Wonderful smells of roasted corn and freshly made tamales filled the plaza. People laughed and music played. Grandpa's large warm hand was holding hers, and Emma felt happy.

El domingo por la tarde, Emma fue con su abuelito al parque. El aire estaba fresco y el sol esplendoroso. La plaza estaba llena de deliciosos aromas de elotes tostados y tamales recién hechos. La gente reía y se oía música. La mano grande y calientita de su abuelito tomaba la suya y Emma se sentía feliz.

But in one corner of the park, people were quiet, listening to a man speak. By his side, his wife held a baby. And by her side were six children, lined up like stair steps.

Emma looked at their clothing, thin and torn, and at their beautiful brown skin, deepened in color by the sun.

"How will I feed my family?" the father asked. "We worked all summer, picking crops. But when it came time to get our pay, the farmer chased us away with a gun! Now we have no food and no place to stay!"

Grandpa saw a flash of lightning in Emma's eyes as she whispered, "But that's not fair, Grandpa!"

Pero en un rincón del parque, la gente estaba callada, escuchando hablar a un hombre. Junto a él, su mujer cargaba un bebé, y a su lado, estaban seis niños parados como si fueran escaloncitos.

Emma observó su ropa desgarrada y su linda piel morena, quemada por el sol.

—¿Cómo le daré de comer a mi familia? —preguntó el papá. —Trabajamos todo el verano, piscando. Pero a la hora de recibir el pago, ¡el dueño nos corrió con una escopeta! ¡Ahora no tenemos ni casa ni comida!

El abuelito vio en los ojos de Emma un relámpago, mientras ella susurraba —¡Pero eso no es justo, abuelito!

That night, Grandpa poured a cup of frothy hot chocolate for Emma. Then Grandpa held her in his arms.

Emma told him about the cold baby, about the hungry little boys, and why María couldn't read. Her words tumbled out as if they had been shut inside her.

"It's not fair!" she sobbed. Grandpa listened, and her words touched the depths of his heart.

Esa noche, su abuelito batió una taza de chocolate espumoso y calientito para Emma. Y la acurrucó en sus brazos.

Emma le contó del bebé que tenía frío, de los niñitos que tenían hambre, y de María que nunca aprendió a leer. Sus palabras brotaron como si hubieran estado encerradas en ella.

—¡No es justo! —sollozó Emma. Y sus palabras llegaron al fondo del corazón de su abuelito.

The next day, Emma and Grandpa went for a walk. They passed large, handsome houses and tiny shacks. From both, people smiled and waved at them.

18

Al siguiente día, Emma y su abuelito salieron a caminar. Pasaron por donde había casas grandes y elegantes, y casuchas muy chiquitas. Todos les saludaban y sonreían.

They walked on, and saw people hard at work.
Some were going into dark, dreary factories
to shell pecans. Some entered elegant buildings.

Vieron personas trabajando con toda su fuerza.
Algunas entraban a oscuras maquiladoras a pelar
nueces; otras, a edificios elegantes.

They saw a man so old he could hardly walk. But he cradled a guitar in his arms and sang. The words sounded so beautiful that his rich voice almost didn't need the melody.

Sol que eres tan parejo
para repartir tu luz,
habrías de enseñarle al amo
pa' qu'él sea igual que tú.

Emma smiled as she repeated the words to herself:
     "Sun," the song said, "you are so even, so fair, as you share your light so equally with everyone. You should teach my boss to be as fair as you."

Vieron a un hombre tan anciano que ya no podía caminar. Pero llevaba en sus brazos una guitarra y cantaba. Las palabras eran tan bellas que su voz vieja ni necesitaba de la melodía.

Sol que eres tan parejo
para repartir tu luz,
habrías de enseñarle al amo
pa' qu'él sea igual que tú.

Una sonrisa pasó por los labios de Emma, mientras repetía las palabras para sí misma.

After the walk, Emma was still humming the song. Again, Grandpa poured hot chocolate into Emma's favorite cup.

As she drank the soothing cinnamon chocolate, Grandpa said, "Sometimes things are not fair. But still, each one of us can usually do something about it, even if it's just a little thing."

Emma asked, "Like when we gave the man in the park our ice cream money? Maybe he bought milk for the baby? Or the other day when you took me with you to vote for laws to make things fair?"

Grandpa nodded.

"And the old man. He helped, too," said Emma, "by singing a song with the right words to make people understand."

Después de la caminata, Emma todavía tarareaba la canción. Otra vez, su abuelito le sirvió chocolate en su taza favorita.

Mientras ella lo bebía, él dijo: —A veces, las cosas no son justas. Pero cada uno de nosotros puede hacer algo para ayudar, aunque sea una cosa pequeña.

—¿Como cuando le dimos el dinero para comprar nuestros helados al señor en el parque? Quizá pudo comprar leche para el bebé. —comentó Emma. —¿O como el otro día cuando me llevaste contigo para votar por leyes justas?

Su abuelito afirmó con la cabeza.

—Y el viejito; él también ayudó —añadió Emma —cantando las palabras adecuadas que ayudarían a que la gente comprendiera la situación.

The next day, on the way back from school, Emma saw the three young brothers.

"Here," she said, as she handed them an apple from her lunch sack. But she knew it was just one apple. They would finish it before she was around the corner.

Then, Emma saw the young mother with the thin shawl.

"Here," she said, handing her brand new blue sweater to the mother. "It's for the baby."

But she knew that it was just one sweater. It might only last through a winter or two.

Al siguiente día al regresar de la escuela, Emma vio a los tres hermanitos.

—Tengan —les dijo, ofreciéndoles una manzana de su lonchera. Pero era sólo una manzana, y pensó que se la acabarían antes de que ella diera vuelta en la esquina.

Después vio a la madre del rebozo muy gastado.

—Tenga —le dijo, dándole su suéter azul nuevecito. —Es para el bebé.

Pero sabía que era sólo un suéter. Sabía que no duraría muchos inviernos.

27

When she got home, though, she began to teach María letters, words, and how to read.
And this, Emma knew, would last her forever.

Cuando llegó a su casa, comenzó a enseñarle a María letras, palabras y cómo leer.
Y Emma supo que esto le duraría para siempre.

Years passed, and Emma grew into a smart, kind teenager. All around her there was hunger, misery and poverty. And the poorest of all the workers were the pecan shellers. Many were only paid four cents for their best hour of work. Most of them were Mexican-American. Most were women. Some were children.

Emma began to speak to others about things that were not fair. She spoke in public parks and in the market where the farmers sold their vegetables. She even spoke on the steps of city hall!

When she spoke to the people, her dark eyes flashed and her voice was full of courage and caring. The people listened, and her words touched their hearts, sparking hope as bright as lightning in a dark night sky.

Pasaron los años y Emma llegó a ser una adolescente inteligente y cariñosa. Por todos lados veía hambre y miseria. Y de todos los obreros, los más pobres eran los peladores de nuez. Muchos sólo ganaban 4 centavos la hora, aunque trabajaran con muchísima rapidez. La mayoría de ellos eran méxico-americanos. Casi todos eran mujeres. Y algunos niños.

Emma comenzó a hablar en público de las cosas que no eran justas. Habló en los parques y en el mercado donde los campesinos vendían sus vegetales. ¡Habló hasta en los escalones del gobierno municipal!

Cuando decía sus discursos, sus ojos oscuros resplandecían y su voz estaba llena de valentía y de compasión. La gente la escuchaba y sus palabras prendían en el corazón del pueblo una chispa de esperanza tan clara como un relámpago en una noche oscura.

1938 . . .

But many of their bosses would not listen. They wanted to pay the workers as little as they could. When Emma was 21, the bosses decided to drop the pecan shellers' pay even lower. Now they could barely make three cents for an hour of work! The workers feared that their children would starve to death.

Emma was angry.

She saw so many people go to work when it was still dark and not come home again until late at night. Many worked so many hours that they were coughing and sick, and still they did not earn enough to feed their children.

She saw owners work one or two hours a day. They had so much money they would throw away elegant clothing they had used only once, or throw away food that the workers wished they could give their children.

Pero muchos de los dueños no escucharían. Querían pagar a los trabajadores lo menos posible. Cuando Emma tenía 21 años, los dueños decidieron bajar el pago aún más. Ahora los peladores de nuez no podían ganar ni tres centavos la hora. Los trabajadores temían que sus hijos murieran de hambre.

Emma estaba enojada.

Ella veía a innumerables personas que iban a trabajar antes de que saliera el sol y regresaban a sus casas hasta muy noche. Muchos trabajaban tantas horas que estaban enfermos y tosiendo y todavía no ganaban bastante para dar de comer a sus hijos.

Observaba a los dueños que trabajaban una o dos horas al día. Ellos tenían tanto dinero que tiraban ropa cara después de usarla sólo una vez, o desperdiciaban comida que los nueceros hubieran querido dar a sus hijos.

elled pecans
6¢
a pound

She spoke to the owners, begging them to think of the workers.

One owner laughed. "What does it matter that they are poor?" he said. "They are Mexicans!"

Emma knew that was not fair. When the pecan shellers asked her for help, she knew just what to do.

Emma habló con los dueños, rogándoles que pensaran en los trabajadores.

Uno de ellos se rio. —¿Qué importa que sean pobres? —dijo. —¡Son mexicanos!

Ella sabía que eso no era justo. Cuando los peladores de nuez le pidieron ayuda, ella ya sabía qué hacer.

FAIR WAGES!

FAIR WAGES ¡ES JUSTO!

"You must all stop working until the owners listen to you," said Emma.

"We will make a soup kitchen to feed your families. If we all help each other, we can win."

"No one will listen to you!" some people said, laughing at her.

But 12,000 pecan shellers listened. The factories were almost empty. For nearly two months, the businesses made no money. Many of the owners hated Emma for this. She was threatened and jailed repeatedly. But Emma would not stop fighting for justice.

Finally, the owners were forced to raise the workers' pay.

–Hay que parar de trabajar hasta que los patrones escuchen sus quejas –dijo Emma.

–Haremos una cocina común para dar comida a las familias de los nueceros. Si nos ayudamos todos, podremos ganar.

–Nadie te escuchará –dijeron algunos, riéndose de ella.

Pero 12,000 peladores de nuez la escucharon. Las maquiladoras estaban casi vacías. Por casi dos meses, las empresas de nuez no ganaron dinero. Muchos de los dueños odiaban a Emma por esto. La amenazaron y encarcelaron repetidamente. Pero Emma no dejaba de luchar por la justicia.

Al fin, los dueños de las empresas tuvieron que aumentar el pago a sus trabajadores.

It was only one victory, but the story
of the pecan shellers appeared in newspapers
all across the country. Those who had been
powerless had won against unfairness.
People everywhere celebrated.

The poor loved Emma for what she had
done. She had given them a voice and given
them hope. Tomorrow would be brighter
for everyone.

And that, at last, was fair.

Fue sólo una victoria, pero ·
el caso de los nueceros apareció
en periódicos por toda la nación.
Gente sin poder alguno había
ganado contra la injusticia.
Por todos lados celebraron.

Los pobres querían mucho
a Emma por lo que había hecho.
Ella les había dado voz y esperanza.
Mañana sería mejor para todos.

Y eso, al fin, era justo.

Photographs: *Emma with the striking pecan shellers (top left); Emma organizing a protest (middle); Emma leading a rally in front of city hall (at right); Emma at the age of age 15, shortly before her first protest march (below left).*

Emma Tenayuca

Emma Tenayuca was born on December 21, 1916, in San Antonio, Texas. The second of eleven children, Emma went to live with her grandparents at an early age. Her grandfather often took her to the Plaza del Zacate (Milam Park), where many political figures of the early twentieth century and exiles from the Mexican Revolution gave speeches about the plight of poor workers. At 16, Emma became involved with the Labor Movement when she joined a picket line – and was arrested – during a strike against the Finck Cigar Company. By the age of 20, Emma had become General Secretary for ten chapters of the Workers Alliance of America.

Emma was concerned about the extreme poverty and injustice suffered by Mexican-American workers. In 1938, wages for south Texas pecan shellers (nueceros) were cut drastically. Cases of tuberculosis almost doubled among the workers, mostly caused by breathing pecan dust in crowded, closed rooms. Highly respected for her powerful speeches and her negotiation skills, the workers asked Emma to represent them. Thus, at the age of 21, she led the city's 12,000 pecan shellers in a demand for decent wages and better conditions. At several points, well over 8,000 workers actively joined the strike, despite their starvation-level poverty.

Emma was jailed many times and denied work because of her fierce defense of the poor. Always controversial, she was forced to leave San Antonio to get a job where she was less well known. She worked many years, saved money, and put herself through college in San Francisco, CA. Twenty years later, she returned to San Antonio, earned a Masters Degree, and became a reading teacher for migrant children. Emma died in 1999, leaving behind a large extended family, many who loved her and learned from her, and a legacy of social change and commitment to justice.

This book was written by Emma's niece, Ms. Sharyll Teneyuca, and Emma's friend, Dr. Carmen Tafolla, in her memory. The song sung by the old man in the story is a traditional song of migrant farmworkers. In the year 1985, it was recorded on the album *Canciones de mi padre* by Linda Ronstadt.

About the Authors and Illustrator
of *That's Not Fair! / ¡No es justo!*

Dr. Carmen Tafolla is an internationally published writer and a native of San Antonio's West-Side barrios. The author of five books of poetry and many children's stories, short stories and non-fiction works, her most recent books include *Sonnets and Salsa* and *Baby Coyote and the Old Woman / El coyotito y la viejita*, both published by Wings Press. Tafolla holds her Bachelors, Masters and Doctoral degrees in Education, and has taught at universities, opened a dual-language school in San Antonio for gifted and creative children, and presented her work at schools and colleges throughout North America and Europe. In 1999, she earned the "Art of Peace" Award, pesented by the President's Peace Commission of St. Mary's University. The award honors authors with a significant body of literary works that reflect peace, justice, and human understanding. Carmen Tafolla lives in San Antonio, in a 100-year-old house with her husband, children, and many pecan trees.

Ms. Sharyll Teneyuca is a graduate of Rice University and New York University School of Law. She was voted Outstanding Young Lawyer by the San Antonio Young Lawyers Association in 1985 for her work as the founder and director of the Pro Bono Law Project, the first volunteer attorney assistance project for the representation of indigents in civil matters in Bexar County. As a Municipal Court Judge, she created the Community Service Program, providing an alternative to incarceration for citizens unable to pay city fines. Both programs have become an integral part of the San Antonio community. She has endeavored to carry on her Aunt Emma's legacy of compassion for human beings and dedication to justice. A former Legal Aid staff attorney, she practices law (and makes wonderful pecan pralines) in San Antonio, where she lives with her husband and three sons. She is currently at work with co-author Carmen Tafolla on a full biography of Ms. Emma Tenayuca.

Ms. Terry Ybáñez is a painter and printmaker whose work has been exhibited in numerous places throughout the Americas, including at the University of Mexico (Mexico City) and the Galería de la Raza (San Francisco). A respected (and beloved) artist in her hometown of San Antonio, Texas, she has donated a great deal of her time to creating historical murals honoring significant San Antonio women, including Emma Tenayuca. She illustrated two prior books for children: *Hairs/Pelitos* (1994) by Sandra Cisneros, and *Christmas Tree: El Árbol de Navidad* (1997) by Alma Flor Ada. *Booklist* cited Ybáñez for her "bold, energetic paintings;" *Publishers Weekly* praised her work as "a buoyant celebration." Ybáñez holds degrees in Studio Art and in Bilingual/Bicultural Studies. She lives with her husband and two very friendly dogs, surrounded by pecan trees, near San Antonio's 300-year-old Mission San José and the San Antonio River. She teaches art in an inner-city high school.

Book design by Bryce Milligan

That's Not Fair! Emma Tenayuca's Struggle for Justice /
¡No Es Justo! La lucha de Emma Tenayuca por la justicia
© 2008 by Wings Press for
Carmen Tafolla & Sharyll Teneyuca

This publication is made possible in part by generous grants from the City of San Antonio, Office of Cultural Affairs, and the Alice Kleberg Reynolds Foundation. Thanks also to StoneMetal Press and the Esperanza Peace and Justice Center for significant support of this project.

Fourth Printing, 2010

ISBN-10: 0-916727-33-5
ISBN-13: 978-0-916727-33-8

Wings Press
627 E. Guenther, San Antonio, Texas 78210
Phone/fax: (210) 271-7805

On-line catalogue and ordering:
www.wingspress.com
All Wings Press titles are distributed to the trade by
Independent Publishers Group
www.ipgbook.com

Library of Congress Cataloging-in-Publication Data

Tafolla, Carmen, 1951- and Teneyuca, Sharyll
    That's not fair! : Emma Tenayuca's struggle for justice = No es justo! : la lucha de Emma Tenayuca por la justicia / written by Carmen Tafolla & Sharyll Teneyuca ; illustrated by Terry Ybáñez ; Spanish translation by Carmen Tafolla.
      p. cm.
    ISBN-13: 978-0-916727-33-8 (hardcover : alk. paper)
    ISBN-10: 0-916727-33-5 (hardcover : alk. paper)
    1. Tenayuca, Emma, 1916-1999--Juvenile literature. 2. Labor leaders--United States--Biography--Juvenile literature. 3. Women labor leaders--United States--Biography--Juvenile literature. I. Teneyuca, Sharyll. II. Ybáñez, Terry. III. Title. IV. Title: No es justo!
    HD6509.T46T34 2008
    331.88092--dc22
    [B]   2007033343

Printed in China